Alfred's Basic Piano Library

Solo Book • Complete Levels 2

P *i a n* o

Selected and Edited by E. L. Lancaster & Morton Manus

This new series answers the often expressed need for a variety of supplementary material in many different popular styles. What could be more fun for a young student than to play the music that everybody knows and loves? The remarkable part of this new *Top Hits* series is that soon after beginning piano study, young students can play attractive versions of the best-known music of today.

This book is correlated page-by-page with Lesson Book Complete Levels 2 & 3 of Alfred's Basic Piano Library; pieces should be assigned based on the instructions in the upper-right corner of each title page of *Top Hits*.

Since the melodies and rhythms of popular music do not always lend themselves to precise grading, you may find that these pieces are sometimes a little more difficult than the corresponding pages in the Lesson Book. The teacher's judgment is the most important factor in deciding when to begin each title.

When the books in the *Top Hits* series are assigned in conjunction with the Lesson Books, these appealing pieces reinforce new concepts as they are introduced. In addition, the motivation the music provides could not be better. The emotional satisfaction students receive from mastering each popular song increases their enthusiasm to begin the next one. With the popular music available in the *Top Hits* series, the use of these books will significantly increase student interest in piano study to successively higher levels.

Published by
HAL•LEONARD®
C O R P O R A T I O N

Distributed by
Alfred Publishing Co., Inc.

ISBN 0-7390-1181-2
All Rights Reserved.   Printed in USA.
Cover photos: Camera, popcorn box © 1999 PhotoDisc, Inc.
Backgrounds, movie clapboard © Eyewire, Inc.

What a Wonderful World

Use with Alfred's Basic Piano Library,
LESSON BOOK Complete Levels 2 & 3,
after page 5.

Words and Music by
George David Weiss and Bob Thiele
Arr. by George Peter Tingley

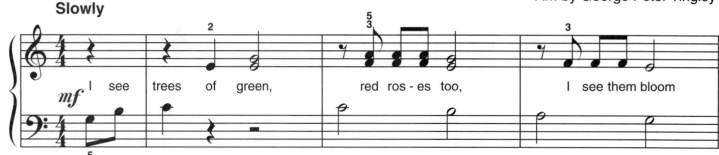

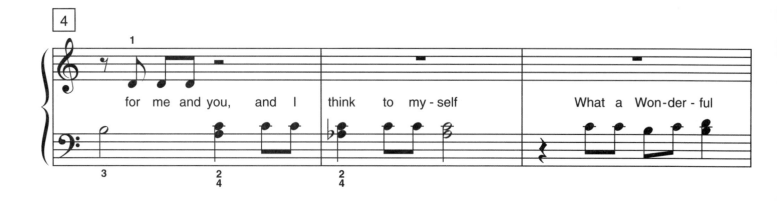

DUET PART (Student plays one octave higher than written.)

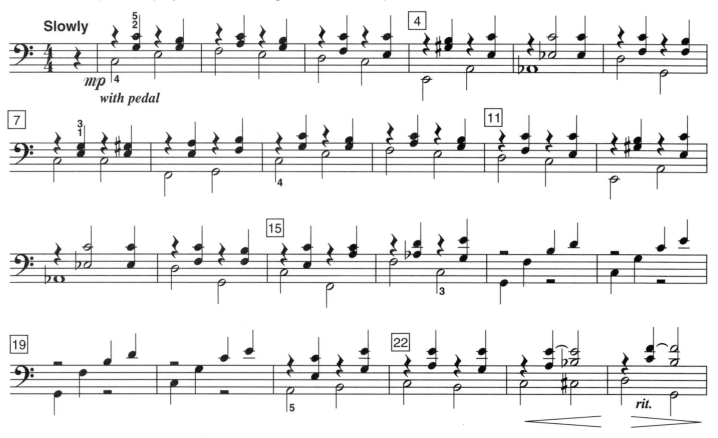

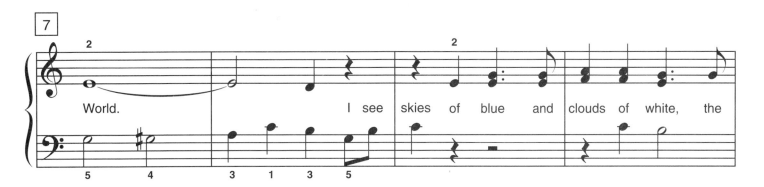

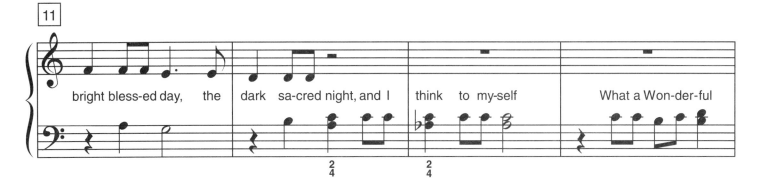

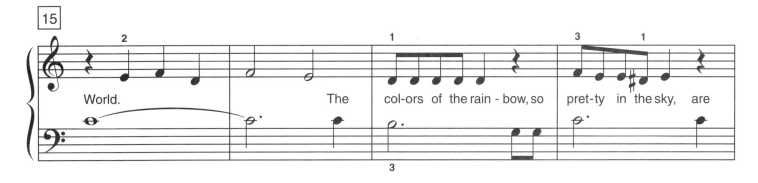

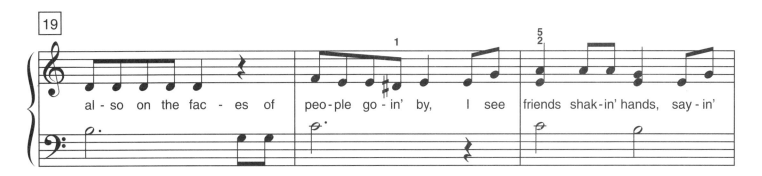

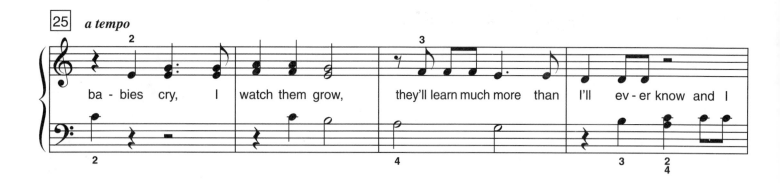

Beauty and The Beast

from Walt Disney's BEAUTY AND THE BEAST

Lyrics by Howard Ashman
Music by Alan Menken
Arr. by Dennis Alexander

Tale as old as time, true as it can be. Bare-ly e-ven

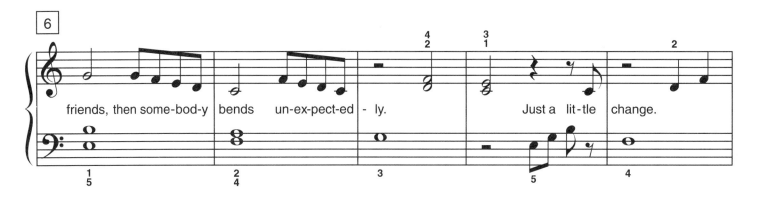

friends, then some-bod-y bends un-ex-pect-ed - ly. Just a lit-tle change.

Small, to say the least. Both a lit-tle scared, nei-ther one pre-pared, Beau-ty and The Beast.

(Move LH 2
down to F)

DUET PART (Student plays one octave higher.)

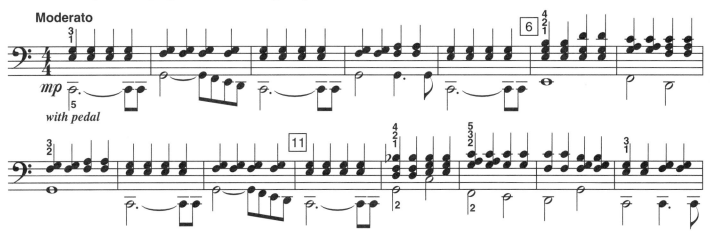

6

Ev-er just the same. Ev-er a sur-prise. Ev-er as be-

(Move LH 5 up to E)

fore,   ev - er just as   sure   as the sun will   rise.   Tale as old as

slower   rit.

8va

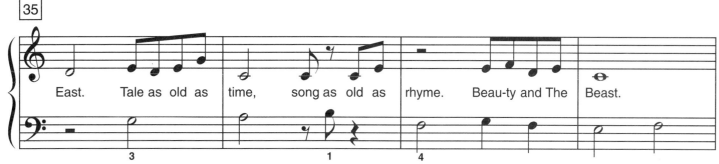

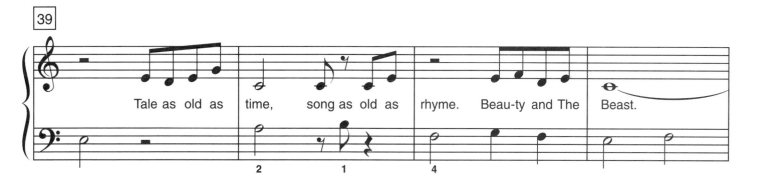

(Move LH 2 down to F)

Use after page 13.

The Grouch Song

from the Television Series SESAME STREET

Words and Music by Jeff Moss
Arr. by Sharon Aaronson

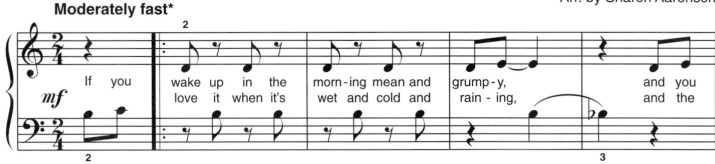

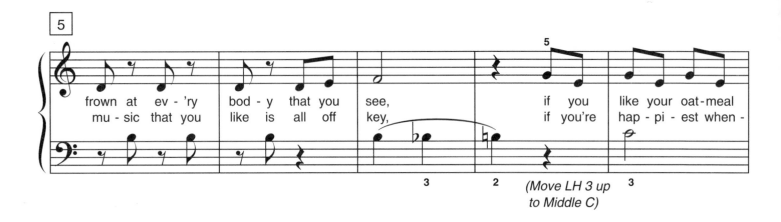

DUET PART (Student plays one octave higher than written.)

*Play eighth notes a bit unevenly, in a "lilting" style: long   short long   short, *etc.*

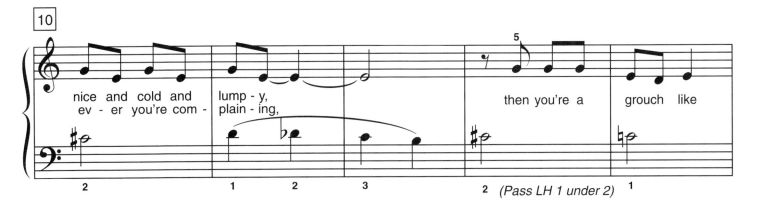

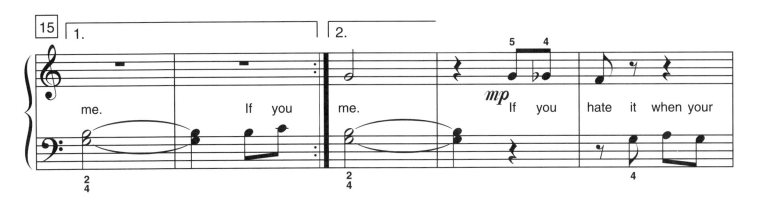

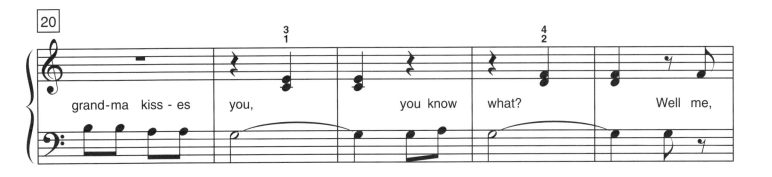

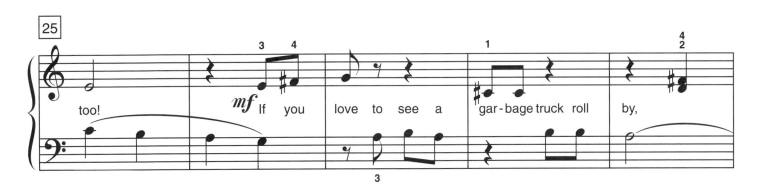

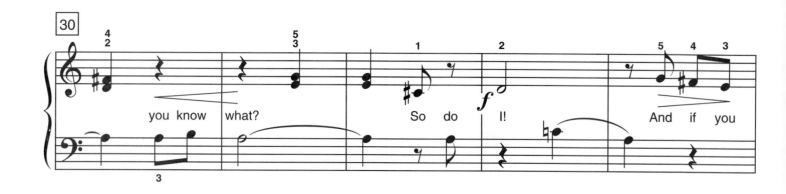

you know what?   So do I!   And if you

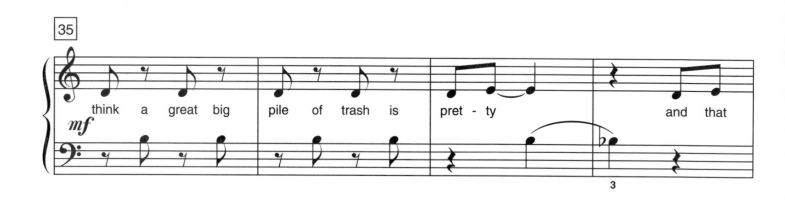

think a great big   pile of trash is   pret - ty   and that

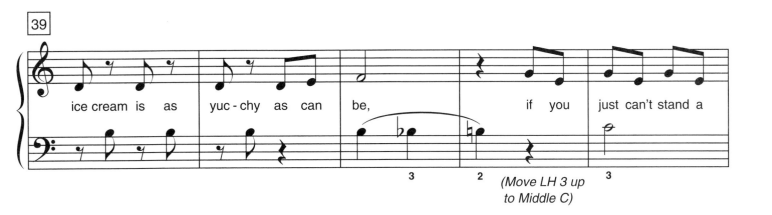

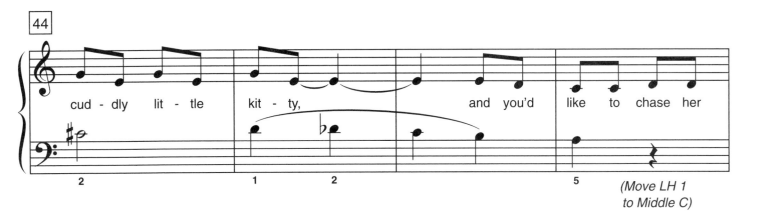

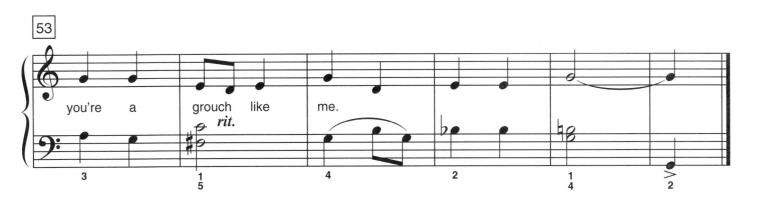

Use after page 17.

The Rainbow Connection

from THE MUPPET MOVIE

By Paul Williams and Kenneth L. Ascher
Arr. by Dennis Alexander

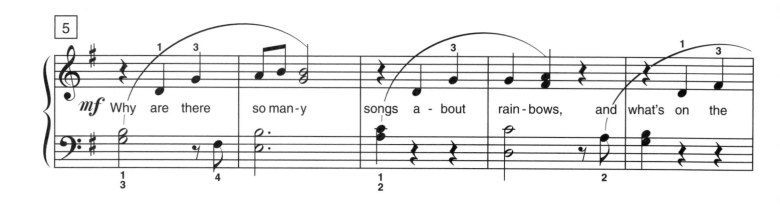

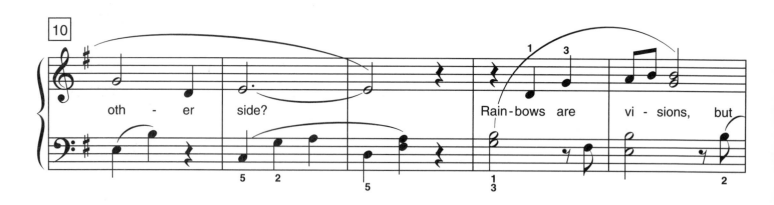

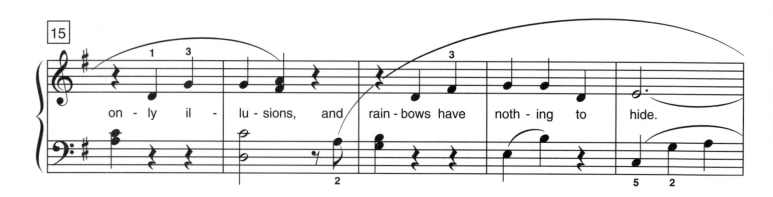

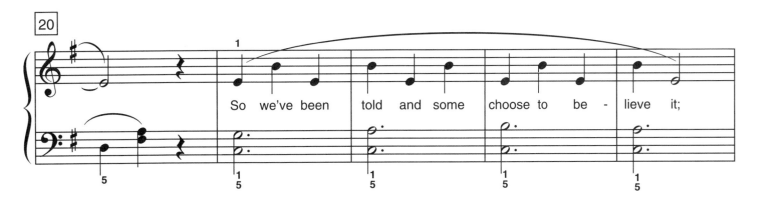

So we've been told and some choose to be - lieve it;

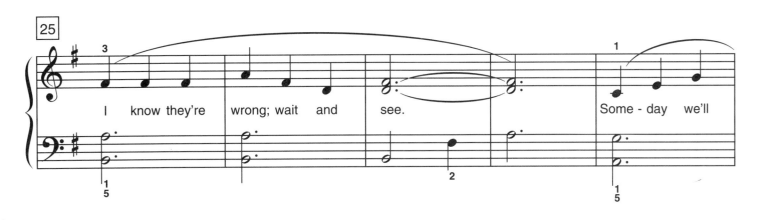

I know they're wrong; wait and see. Some - day we'll

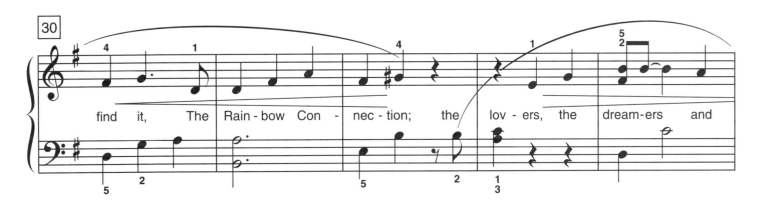

find it, The Rain - bow Con - nec - tion; the lov - ers, the dream-ers and

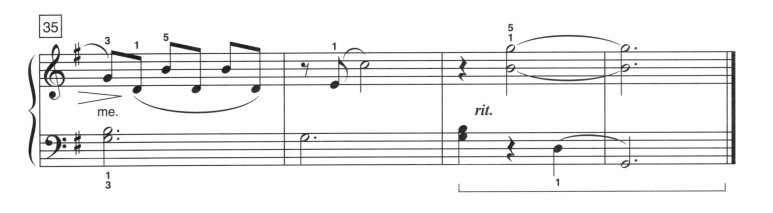

me. *rit.*

Use after page 23.

Won't You Be My Neighbor?

(It's a Beautiful Day In This Neighborhood)

from MISTER ROGERS' NEIGHBORHOOD

Words and Music by Fred Rogers
Arr. by Martha Mier

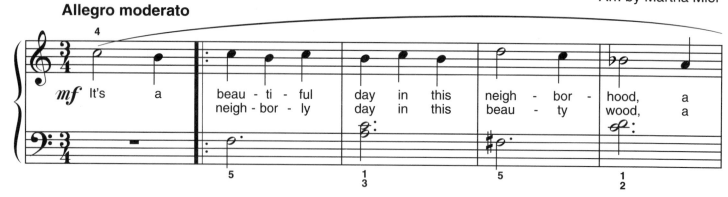

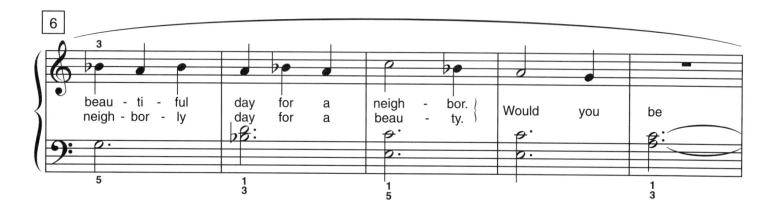

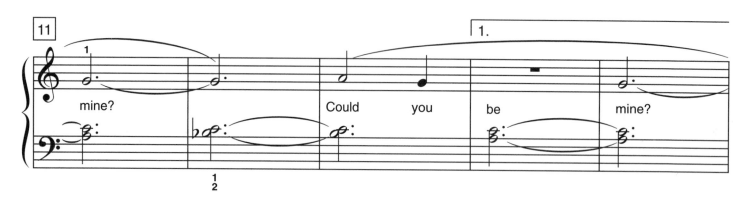

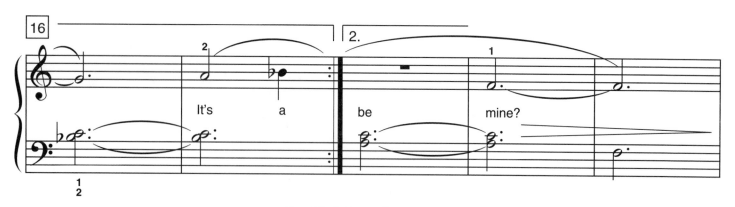

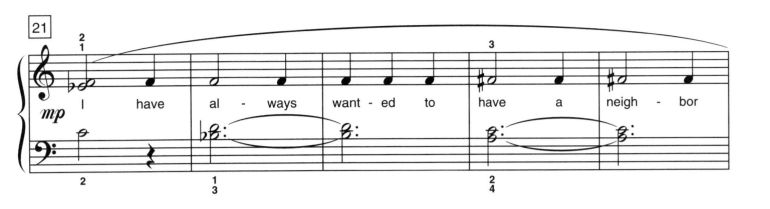

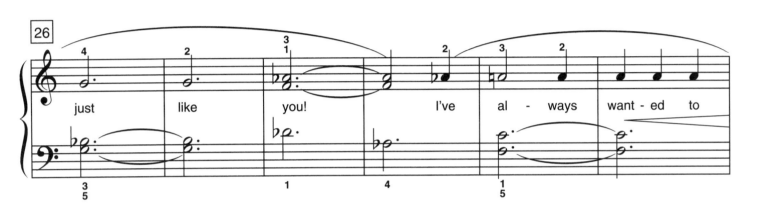

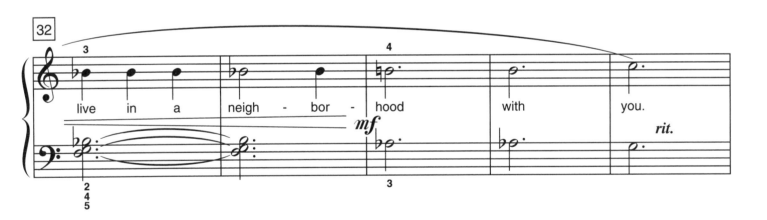

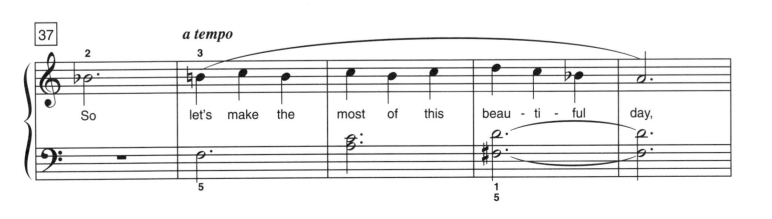

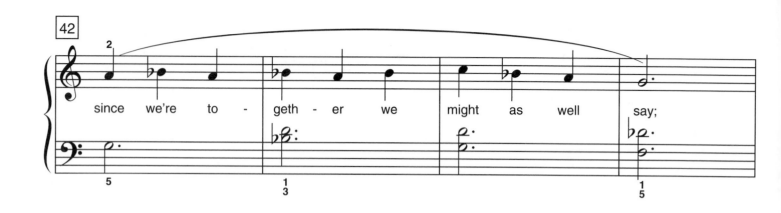

since we're to - geth - er we might as well say;

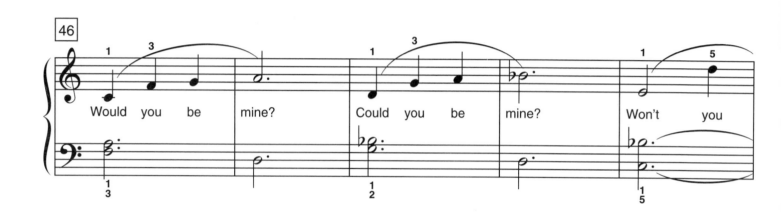

Would you be mine? Could you be mine? Won't you

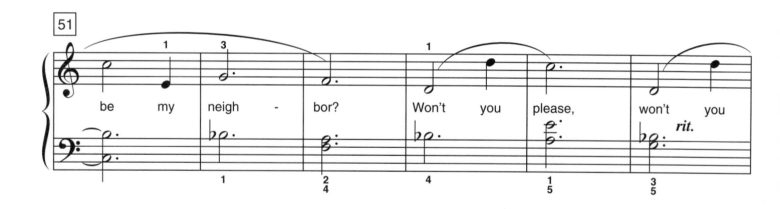

be my neigh - bor? Won't you please, won't you

rit.

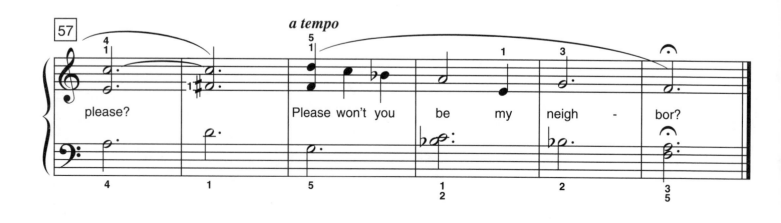

a tempo

please? Please won't you be my neigh - bor?

Can You Feel the Love Tonight

from Walt Disney Pictures' THE LION KING

Music by Elton John
Lyrics by Tim Rice
Arr. by Sharon Aaronson

Slowly, with a steady beat

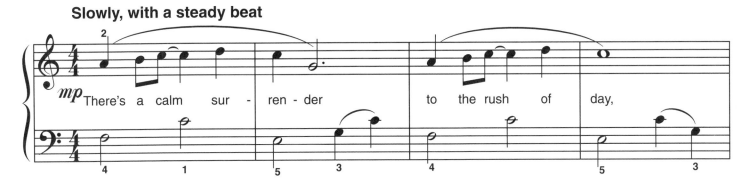

There's a calm sur - ren - der to the rush of day,

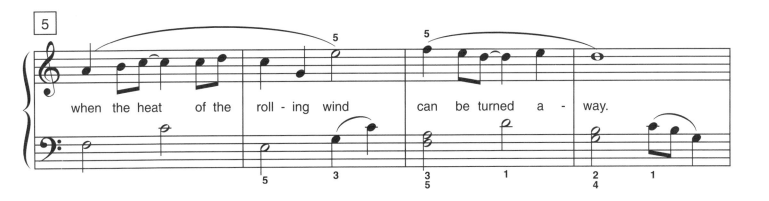

when the heat of the roll - ing wind can be turned a - way.

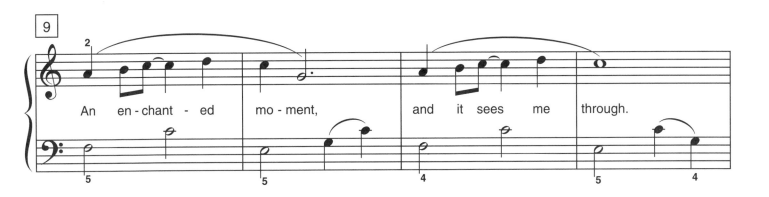

An en - chant - ed mo - ment, and it sees me through.

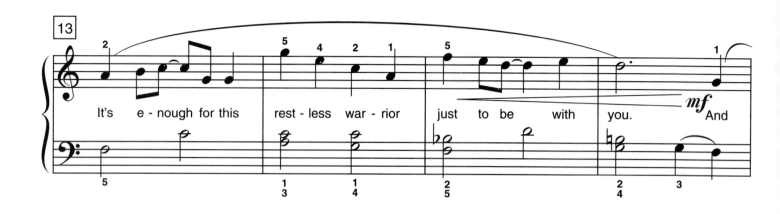

It's e - nough for this rest - less war - rior just to be with you. And

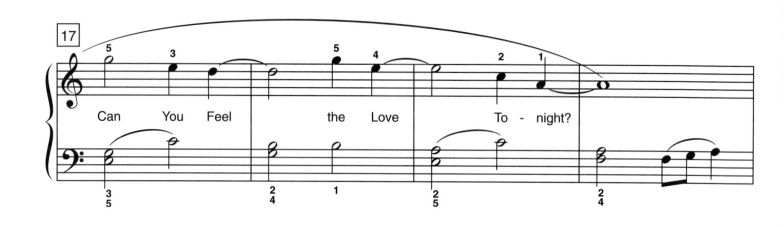

Can You Feel the Love To - night?

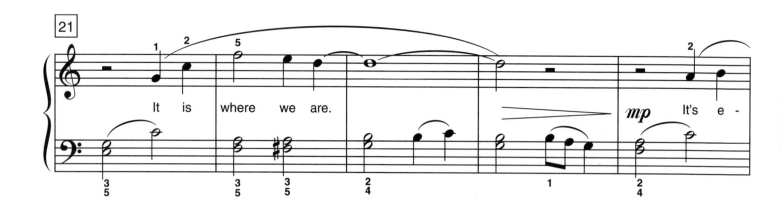

It is where we are. It's e -

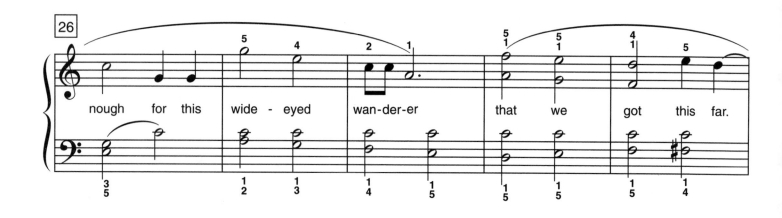

nough for this wide - eyed wan-der-er that we got this far.

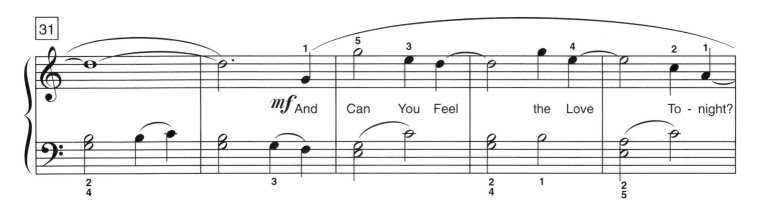

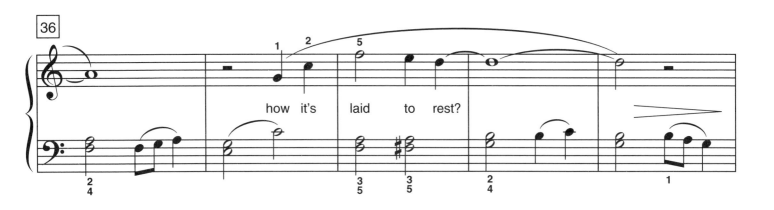

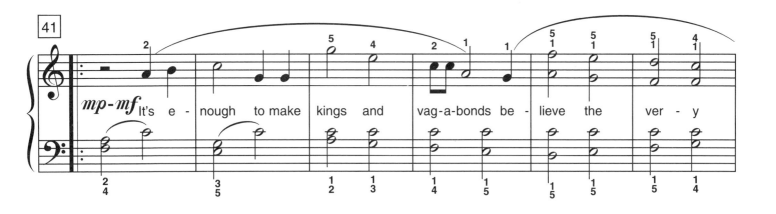

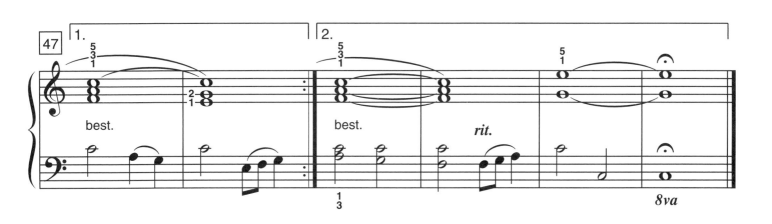

Use after page 31.

Supercalifragilisticexpialidocious

from Walt Disney's MARY POPPINS

Words and Music by
Richard M. Sherman and Robert B. Sherman
Arr. by George Peter Tingley

mf Be - cause I was a - fraid to speak when I was just a lad, me

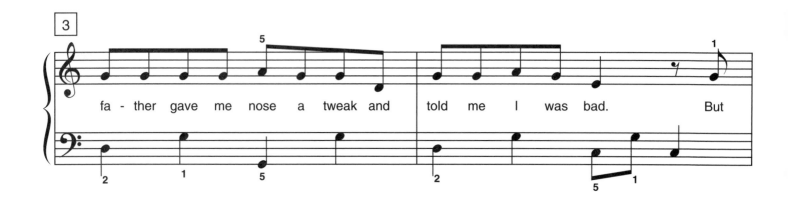

fa - ther gave me nose a tweak and told me I was bad. But

then one day I learned a word that saved me ach - in' nose, the

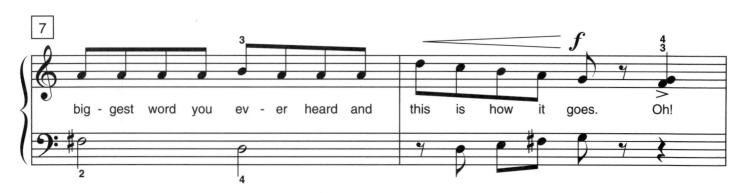

big - gest word you ev - er heard and this is how it goes. Oh!

Use after page 35.

My Favorite Things

from THE SOUND OF MUSIC

Lyrics by Oscar Hammerstein II
Music by Richard Rodgers
Arr. by Christine H. Barden

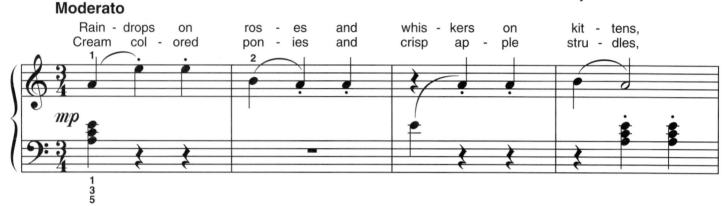

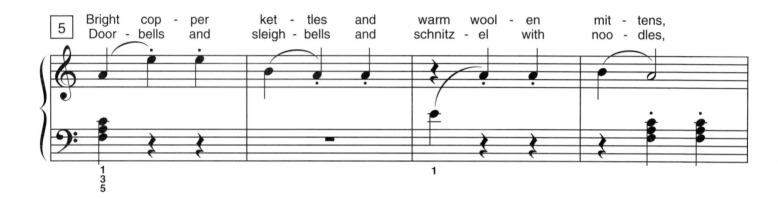

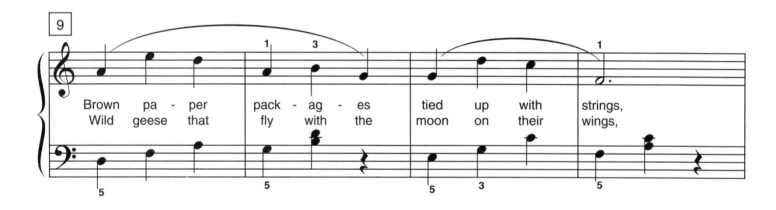

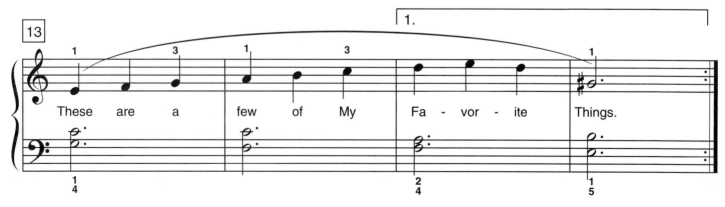

Use after page 35.

Tomorrow

from the Musical Production ANNIE

Lyric by Martin Charnin
Music by Charles Strouse
Arr. by Sharon Aaronson

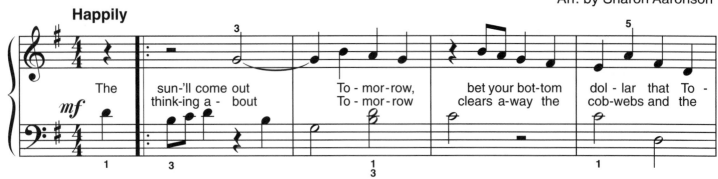

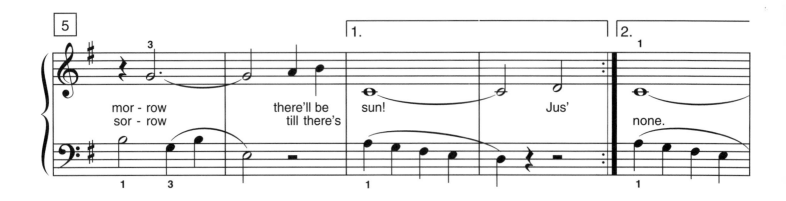

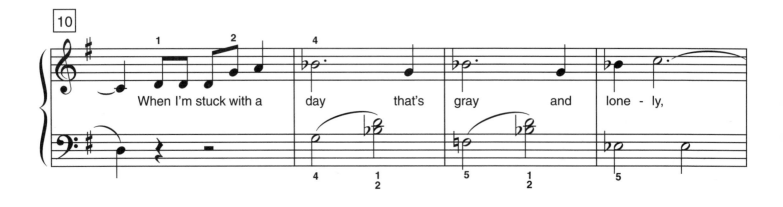

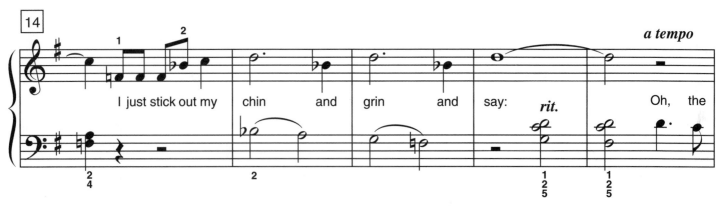

The Bare Necessities

from Walt Disney's THE JUNGLE BOOK

Use after page 39.

Words and Music by Terry Gilkyson
Arr. by George Peter Tingley

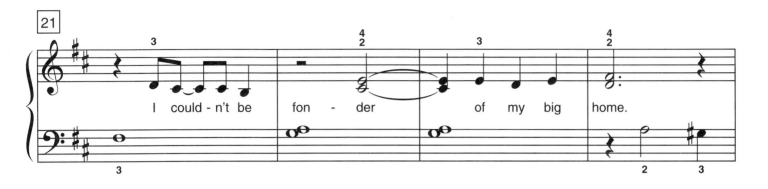

I could - n't be fon - der of my big home.

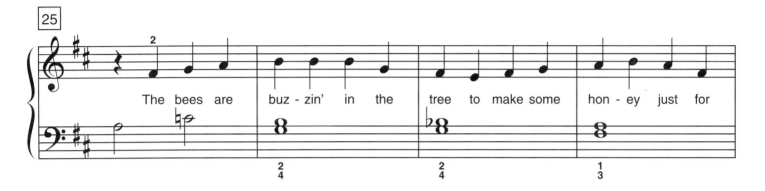

The bees are buz - zin' in the tree to make some hon - ey just for

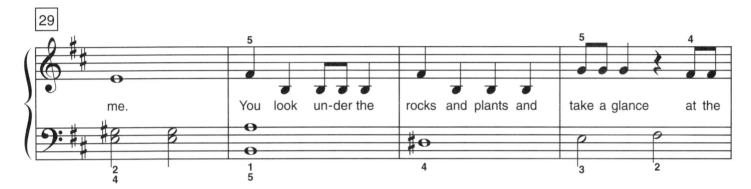

me. You look un-der the rocks and plants and take a glance at the

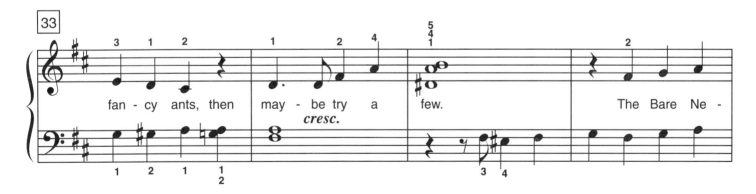

fan - cy ants, then may - be try a few. The Bare Ne -

cresc.

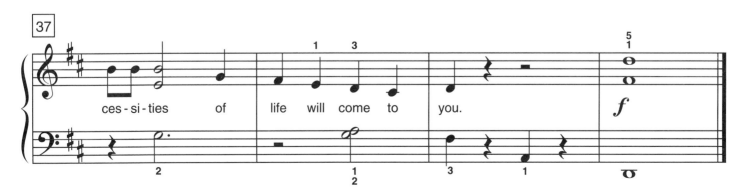

ces - si - ties of life will come to you.

f

Use after page 41.

Part of Your World

from Walt Disney's THE LITTLE MERMAID

Lyrics by Howard Ashman
Music by Alan Menken
Arr. by Tom Gerou

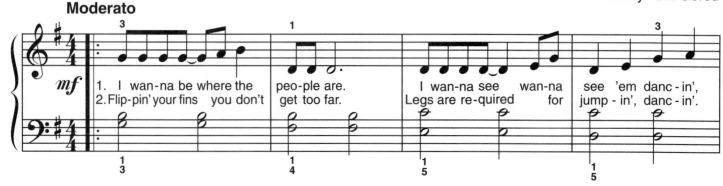

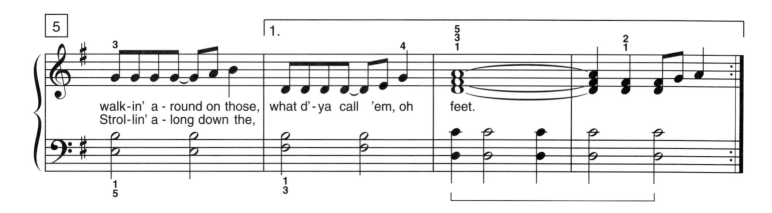

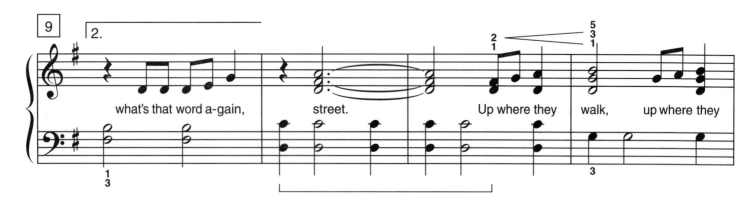

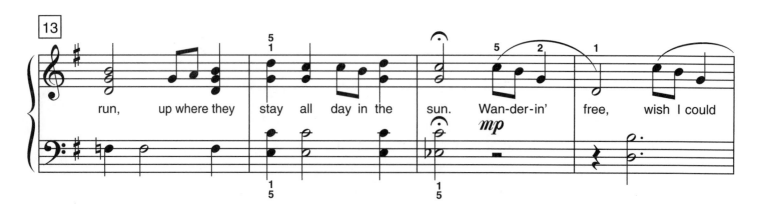

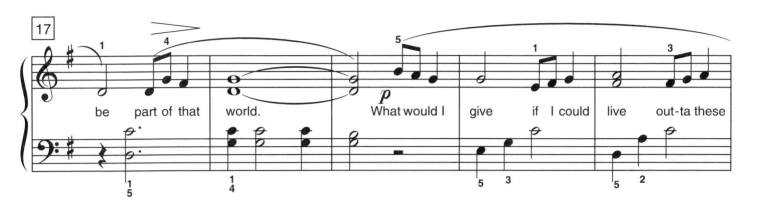

be   part of that   world.   What would I   give   if I could   live   out-ta these

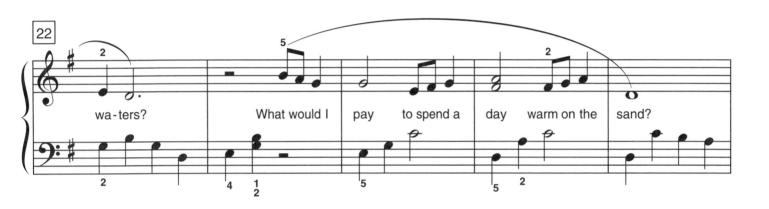

wa-ters?   What would I   pay   to spend a   day   warm on the   sand?

Bet-cha on   land   they un-der - stand.   Bet they don't   re - pri-mand their   daugh-ters. Bright young
cresc.   *mf*   *cresc.*

wom - en,   sick of   swim-min', read-y to   *f* stand.   *mf* And

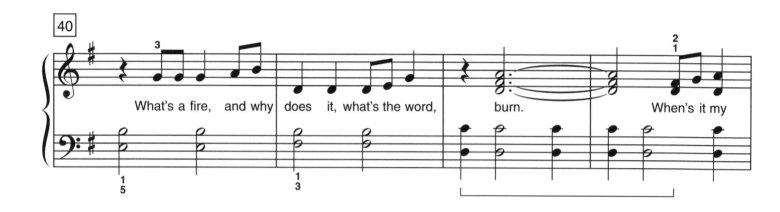

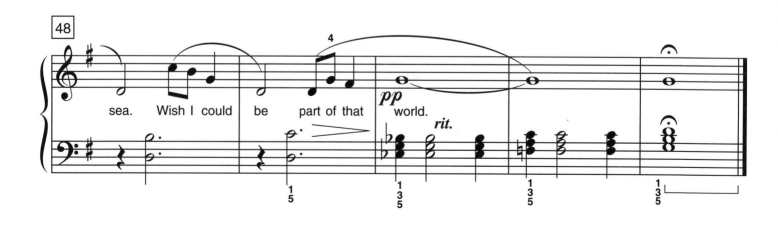

I Just Can't Wait to Be King

from Walt Disney Pictures' THE LION KING

Music by Elton John
Lyrics by Tim Rice
Arr. by Sharon Aaronson

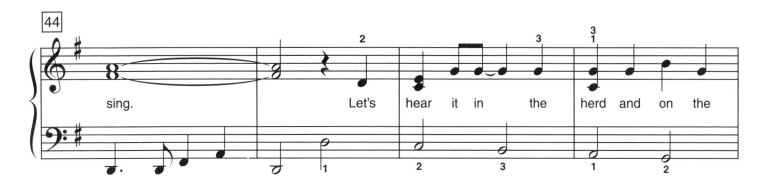

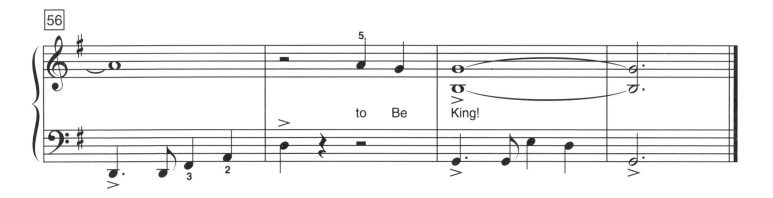

Use after page 49.

My Heart Will Go On (Love Theme from 'Titanic')

from the Paramount and Twentieth Century Fox Motion Picture TITANIC

Music by James Horner
Lyric by Will Jennings
Arr. by George Peter Tingley

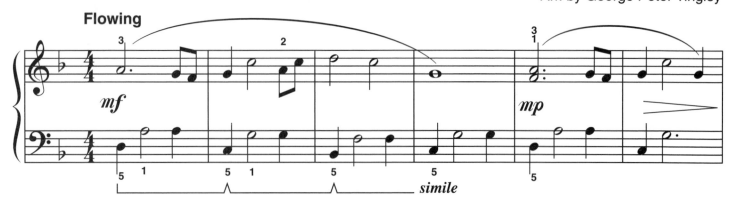

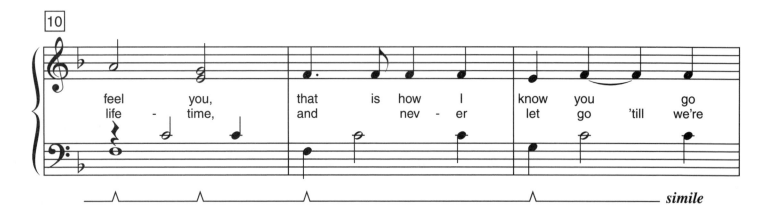

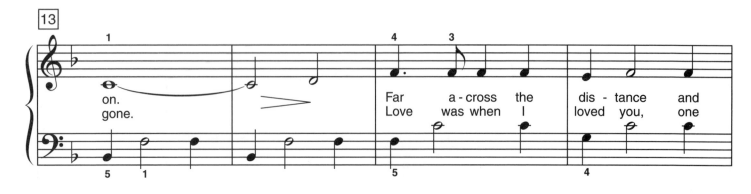

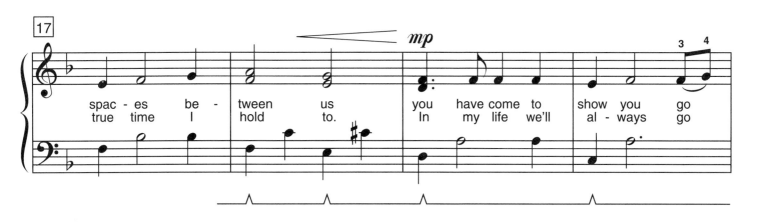

spac - es be - tween us to.
true time I hold to.
you have come to show you go
In my life we'll al - ways go

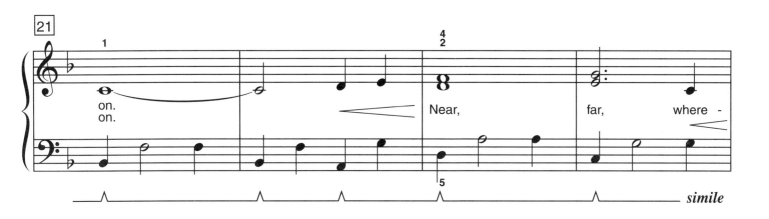

on.
on.
Near, far, where -

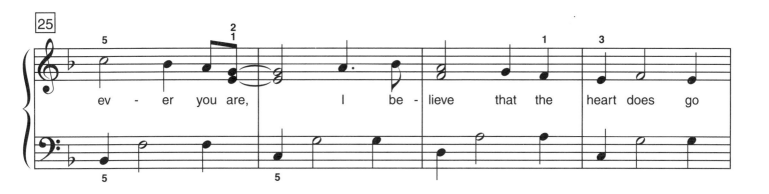

ev - er you are, I be - lieve that the heart does go

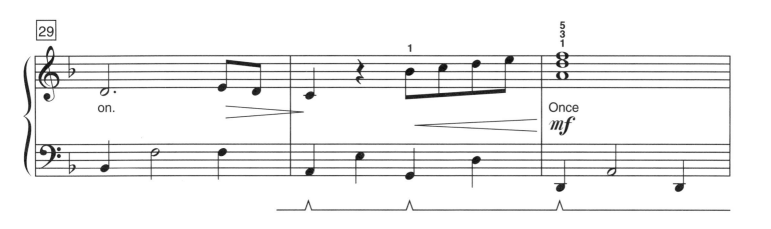

on.
Once

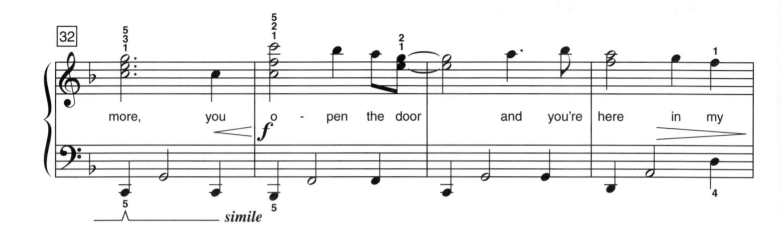

more, you o - pen the door and you're here in my

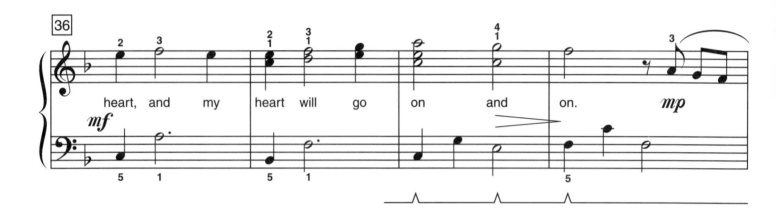

heart, and my heart will go on and on.

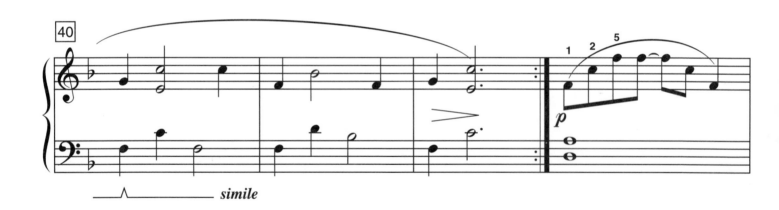

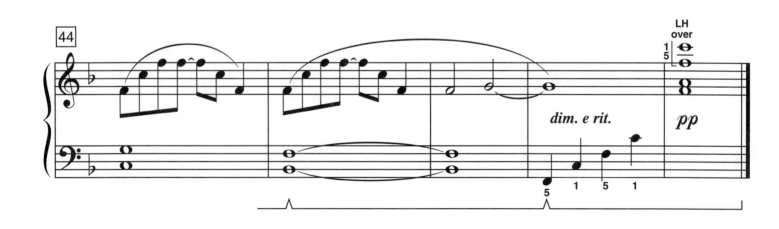

dim. e rit.

A Whole New World

from Walt Disney's ALADDIN

Music by Alan Menken
Lyrics by Tim Rice
Arr. by Dennis Alexander

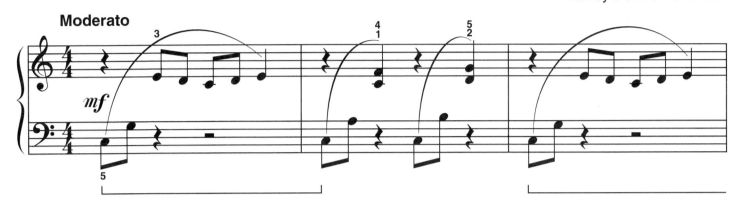

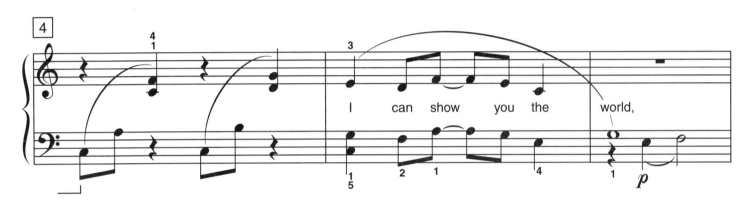

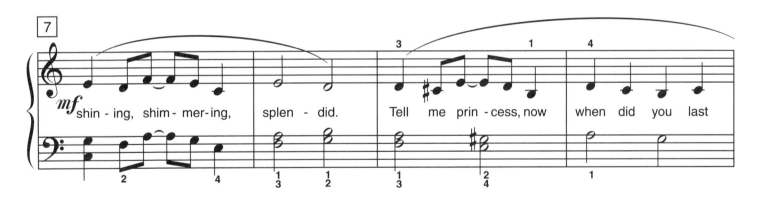

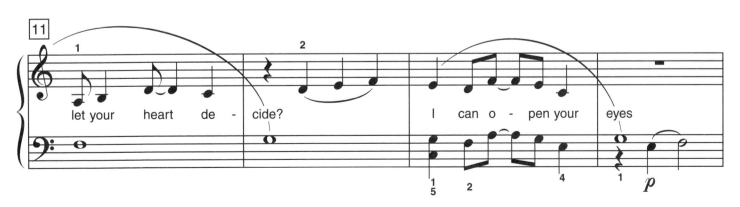

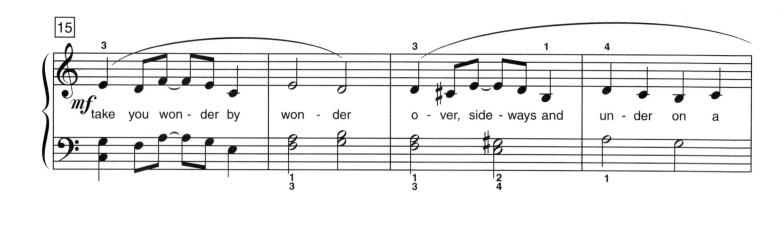

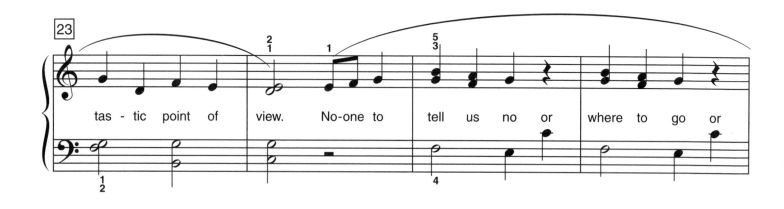

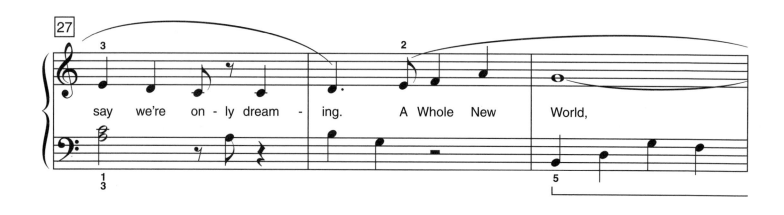

Memory

from CATS

Use after page 61.

Music by Andrew Lloyd Webber
Text by Trevor Nunn after T. S. Eliot
Arr. by Sharon Aaronson

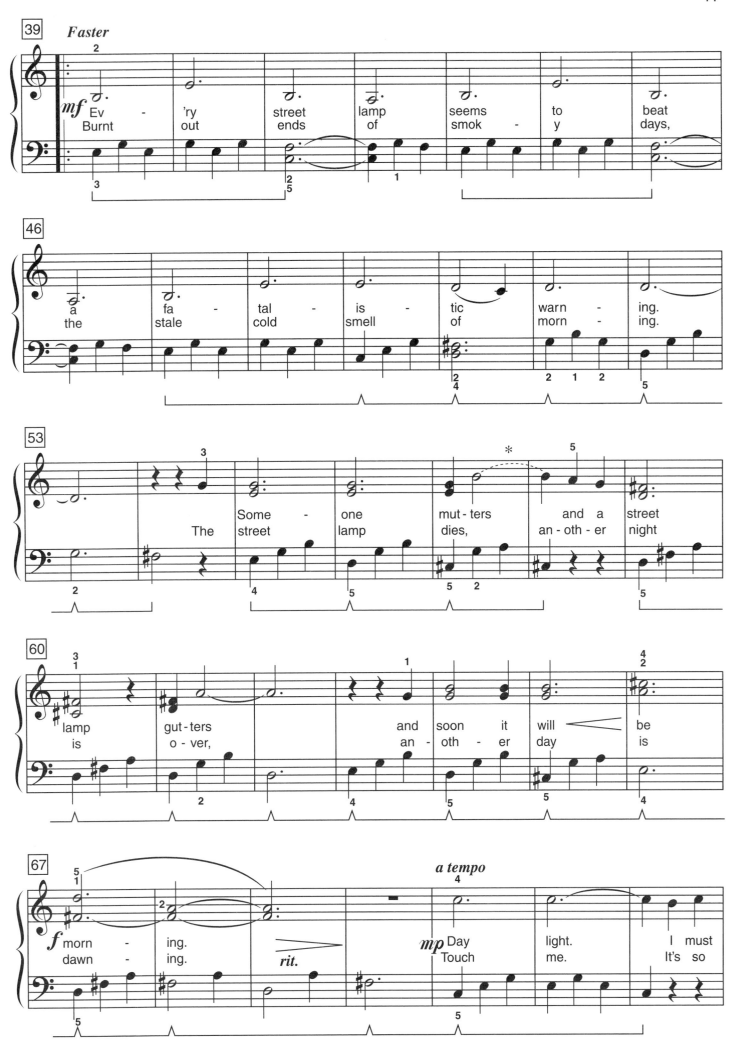

*Tie 1st time only.

42

The Sound of Music

from THE SOUND OF MUSIC

Lyrics by Oscar Hammerstein II
Music by Richard Rodgers
Arr. by Sharon Aaronson

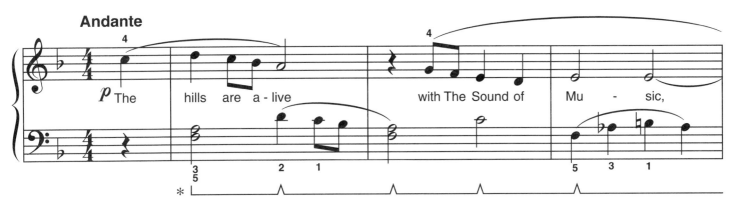

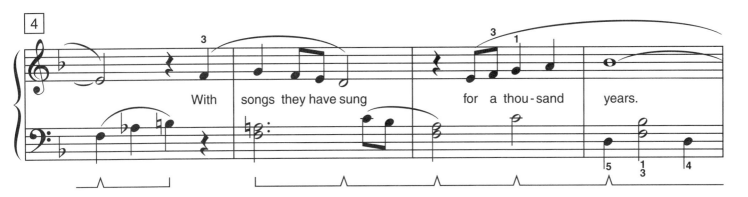

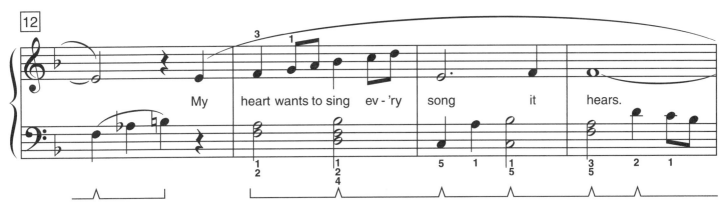

*Pedal optional.

44

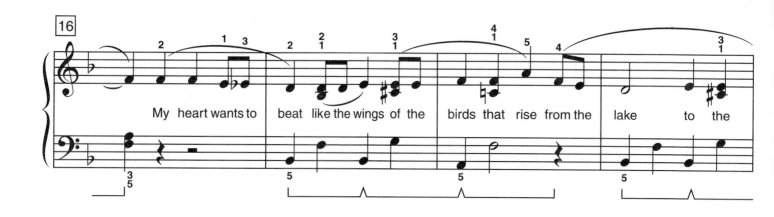

My heart wants to beat like the wings of the birds that rise from the lake to the

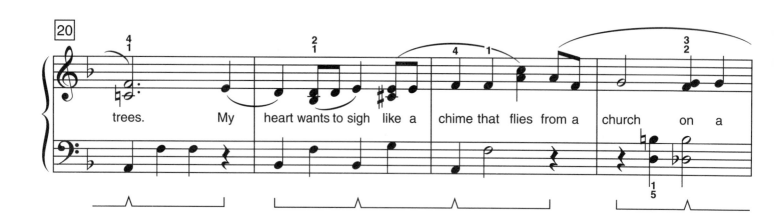

trees. My heart wants to sigh like a chime that flies from a church on a

breeze, *mf* To laugh like a brook when it trips and falls o-ver stones on its

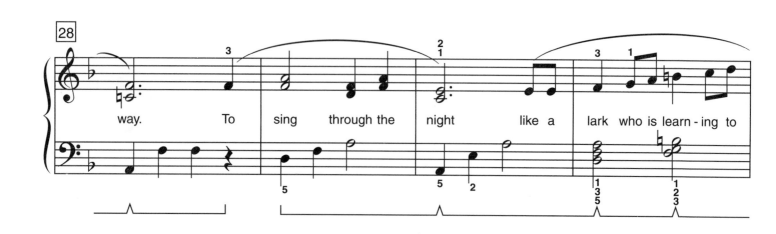

way. To sing through the night like a lark who is learn-ing to

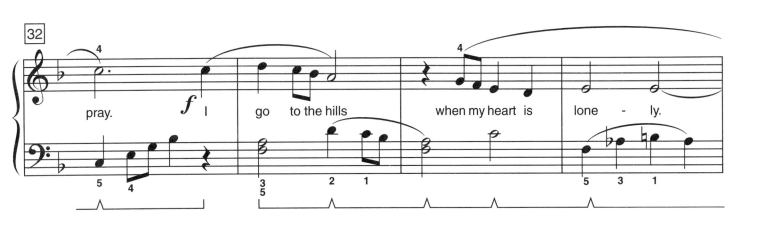

pray.   *f* I   go   to the hills   when my heart is   lone - ly.

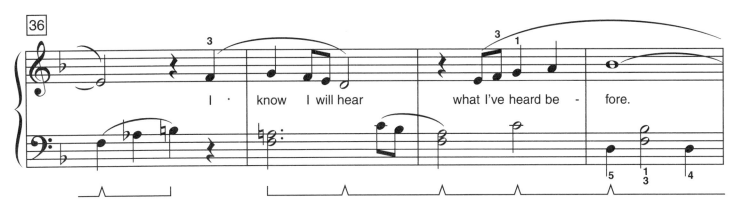

I   know   I will hear   what I've heard be - fore.

ff My   heart will be blessed   with The Sound of   Mu - sic

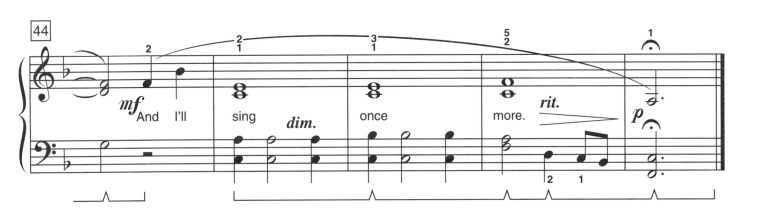

mf And   I'll   sing *dim.* once   more. *rit.*   *p*

Use after page 71.

Cruella De Vil

from Walt Disney's 101 DALMATIANS

Words and Music by Mel Leven
Arr. by Tom Gerou

Slow blues

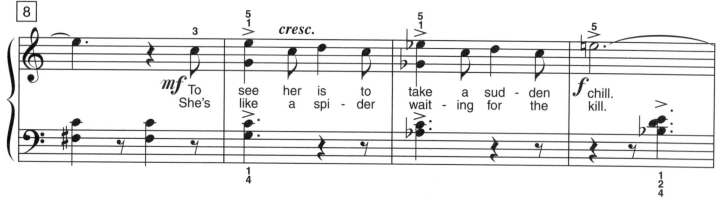

48

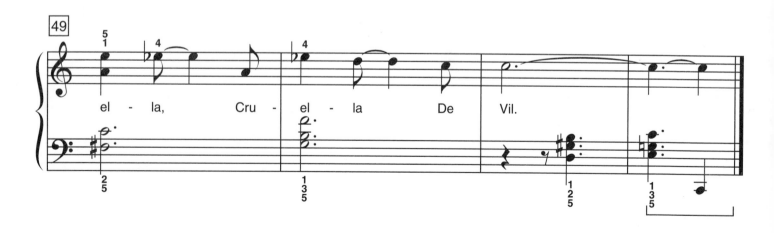